Original title:
Flowing with Passion

Copyright © 2024 Swan Charm
All rights reserved.

Editor: Jessica Elisabeth Luik
Author: Aron Pilviste
ISBN HARDBACK: 978-9916-86-312-1
ISBN PAPERBACK: 978-9916-86-313-8

Mystical Surge

In the heart of twilight's grace,
Whispers dance on moonlit streams.
Silent stars in cosmic chase,
Illuminate the dreamer's dreams.

Waves of wonder crash ashore,
Echoes from the ages past.
Secret realms and hidden lore,
In their grasp, the shadows cast.

Ancient trees with roots so deep,
Guard the tales of time and space.
Through the silence, spirits sweep,
Leaving traces none erase.

Mystic winds through valleys weave,
Carrying the phantom's sighs.
Those who listen can perceive,
Ancient truths and worldly ties.

In this surge of magic's flow,
Mysteries unfold their light.
Every heart begins to know,
The hidden realms beyond our sight.

Seas of Longing

Waves crash with whispered dreams,
Under the moon's soft gleams,
Oceans of hopes unseen,
In waters deep and green.

Echoes in salt-kissed air,
Longings laid bold and bare,
Currents of time do weave,
Tales the hearts believe.

Eddies of the Soul

In whirlpools of deep thought,
Battles unseen are fought,
The mind a restless sea,
Yearning for harmony.

Spirals of love and pain,
Caught in the endless rain,
Questions in silent prose,
Seek what the heart well knows.

Pulse of the Tide

The shore breathes in and out,
With waves, it dances about,
Rhythms of life, unbound,
In the ocean's endless sound.

Heartbeats aligned with moon,
Sands shift ever so soon,
Nature's constant embrace,
Time's unyielding grace.

Rush of the Heart

Feelings like rivers fly,
Beneath the vast, blue sky,
Passions in torrents flow,
In love's sweet undertow.

Moments like stars do gleam,
In every whispered dream,
Desires in swift currents,
Find joy in sentiments.

Cascade of Feelings

A heart in flight, emotions cascade,
Whispers through the soul pervade.
In twilight's glow, a tender serenade,
Echoes of love, the night invade.

Tears of joy, a river wide,
Flow through time, with fervent stride.
Dreams alight, together we confide,
In each other's arms, our worlds collide.

Whirlwind Affection

Whirlwind hearts in passion's storm,
Twining close to keep us warm.
Eyes that sparkle, pure and norm,
In lover's gaze, we transform.

Fleeting moments stretched in time,
Rhythms beating, perfect rhyme.
Lives entwined, a dance sublime,
Hearts aligned, love's paradigm.

Ripples of Ardor

Ripples spread from a love-sweet touch,
In silent waves, they mean so much.
A sigh, a look, no words as such,
Hearts converse in wisdom's clutch.

Gentle notes on love's guitar,
Echo deep from near to far.
Stars align, as they are,
Guiding us, like a lodestar.

Stream of Devotion

Flows of tenderness, a stream so pure,
Carving paths through hearts demure.
In every smile, love's allure,
Binding souls, strong and sure.

Caressing dreams, a gentle stream,
Nurturing hope, like a sunbeam.
Forever bound, not just a theme,
Life unfolds in love's grand scheme.

Waves of Zeal

In the dawn, a cry is heard,
A seagull's call to the horizon's light.
Waves of zeal, fervent and unblurred,
Crash with passion and take flight.

Hearts awakened, dreams unfold,
In surging tides of endless force.
On this ocean, brave and bold,
We sail a true and fearless course.

In the moon's soft, glowing gaze,
A dance of shadows on the crest.
Waves in fervent, endless praise,
Yearning hearts shall never rest.

Ebb and Enthusiasm

The shoreline whispers gentle tales,
Of dreams that ebb and flows renew.
In the heart where passion sails,
An enthusiasm pure and true.

Morning light on waters clear,
Reflects our hopes, both large and small.
In each ripple, far or near,
Lives a fervor, standing tall.

When the evening comes to rest,
And stars illuminate the sky.
In the ebb, we find our best,
In waves of zeal, we're born to fly.

Rapids of Devotion

Through canyons deep and valleys wide,
Rapids rush in swift devotion.
Love's torrent, wild with pride,
Guided by a silent motion.

Hearts that beat in synchrony,
Daring cliffs, their love proclaim.
In the rapids, strong and free,
They forge paths no one can tame.

To the river's endless song,
In devotion, souls confined.
Through life's journey, bound as one,
In the rapids, love will shine.

Swell of the Heart

Beneath the moon, the tides do rise,
A swell within the ocean's heart.
In the depths, the passion lies,
In every beat, a work of art.

Whispers soft on midnight breeze,
Stir emotions deep and true.
In the swell of hearts like these,
Love asserts its gentle hue.

Through each wave, a hand does reach,
Grasping dreams with every start.
In the swell, our souls beseech,
To never let this passion part.

Torrent Hearts

In the echoes of morrow's dawn,
Our hearts as torrents burst and sway,
In currents wild, both dusk and day,
Love's fierce torrents never withdrawn.

Rivers carving rocks anew,
With every beat, with each embrace,
The torrent hearts a fiery chase,
Passions fierce, they're strong and true.

Within the surge of stormy tides,
We navigate the roaring seas,
Two hearts entwined, a love that frees,
That in the torrent still abides.

Fierce Streams

Beneath the stars, the streams so fierce,
They wind through valleys of the soul,
Their passion flow, they seek the goal,
Of hearts they hold and never pierce.

The rush of waters, pure and wild,
Their rhythm like a lover's sigh,
As fierce streams chase the endless sky,
Two souls as one, both free and mild.

In every twist of stream we see,
The depth and breadth of love's expanse,
Through fierce streams' dance, a true romance,
And nothing else shall ever be.

Passionate Currents

With every wave, the currents strong,
They carry us through night and day,
Their song of love, a fervent play,
Where we belong, both right and wrong.

The passionate currents, winding deep,
They carve through hearts with gentle care,
In waters blest, we bravely dare,
A love forever ours to keep.

As currents pull us ever near,
Our hearts beat in a wondrous race,
No fear shall touch this sacred space,
In passionate currents, crystal clear.

Emotive Gush

In emotive gush, hearts' rivers sing,
Through canyons carved by years and tears,
Their love flows deep, dispelling fears,
As every drop begins to cling.

Where waterfalls of feeling start,
They rush into the great unknown,
These emotions, vividly grown,
Emotive gush that pulls the heart.

In swirls of passion, tides embrace,
A torrent of our deepest dreams,
The gush of love in flowing streams,
Together, always face to face.

River's Embrace

In twilight's gentle, soft embrace,
The river flows with tender grace.
Whispers of secrets, tales untold,
In currents deep, their stories unfold.

A dance of shadows on the shore,
Their fleeting forms forever more.
With every ripple, dreams take flight,
Lost in the river's endless night.

The stars above, a mirrored gleam,
Reflecting on the water's dream.
In nature's arms, we find our place,
Within the river's calm embrace.

Waves of Heartbeat

Upon the waves, my heart does beat,
A rhythm strong, both wild and sweet.
Tides of passion, rise and fall,
In love's expanse, I give my all.

The moonlight casts a silver hue,
On waters changed by twilight's view.
Each crest a promise, each trough a sigh,
Within these waves, our spirits fly.

Beneath the skies, both vast and free,
Our love's a stormy, endless sea.
Let every wave, each heartbeat's race,
Unite us in this boundless space.

Rivulets of Ecstasy

In rivulets of ecstasy,
We find a world of harmony.
Where passion flows like liquid gold,
In tales of love, both brave and bold.

Through canyons deep and valleys wide,
In whispered streams, our secrets hide.
The touch of water, gentle, free,
Ignites the flames of ecstasy.

As nature's song within us swells,
In every drop, a magic dwells.
We'll follow where the currents lead,
Our hearts' desire, our souls' pure creed.

Ebbing Heartbeats

In the silence of the evening's fall,
I hear your heartbeat's gentle call.
An ebb and flow, a steady beat,
A rhythm true, so bittersweet.

Through time's embrace, we'll drift away,
Yet heartbeats mark the passage, stay.
Each pulse a memory, moments dear,
A testament of love sincere.

As stars ignite the velvet skies,
Our love remains, it never dies.
In ebbing heartbeats, lives a song,
A melody we've known so long.

Passionate Currents

With every wave, the currents strong,
They carry us through night and day,
Their song of love, a fervent play,
Where we belong, both right and wrong.

The passionate currents, winding deep,
They carve through hearts with gentle care,
In waters blest, we bravely dare,
A love forever ours to keep.

As currents pull us ever near,
Our hearts beat in a wondrous race,
No fear shall touch this sacred space,
In passionate currents, crystal clear.

Emotive Gush

In emotive gush, hearts' rivers sing,
Through canyons carved by years and tears,
Their love flows deep, dispelling fears,
As every drop begins to cling.

Where waterfalls of feeling start,
They rush into the great unknown,
These emotions, vividly grown,
Emotive gush that pulls the heart.

In swirls of passion, tides embrace,
A torrent of our deepest dreams,
The gush of love in flowing streams,
Together, always face to face.

Ebullient Love

In the garden of your heart, I find peace,
Whispers of joy that never cease.
Through the tender glow of morning mist,
Our souls in ebullient love persist.

Beneath the canopy of stars so bright,
We embrace the dawn, igniting the night.
With every touch, our spirits intertwine,
Bound in love, your heart is mine.

Ebullient laughter fills the air,
A symphony of love beyond compare.
Hand in hand, we face the world,
In each other's arms, our love unfurled.

Crimson Stream

Upon the mountains high and steep,
Runs a crimson stream so deep.
Whispers of memories etched in time,
Flowing in rhythm, a silent rhyme.

Beneath the bridge where shadows play,
The stream of dreams finds its way.
Crimson tides of passion and pain,
Washing away sorrow's lingering stain.

In the twilight's soft embrace,
The stream reflects your tender grace.
As night descends, we start to dream,
Carried away by the crimson stream.

Love's Torrent

Like a torrent, wild and free,
Our love flows with fierce decree.
From mountain peaks to ocean's shore,
In your arms, I yearn for more.

Love's tempest, fierce and bold,
Stories of passion, yet untold.
Amidst the chaos, hearts take flight,
Bound by love, day and night.

In the storm, we find our calm,
Embraced within love's healing balm.
With every wave, our spirits soar,
Together forever, forevermore.

Zephyr of Ecstasy

Through the fields, where wildflowers bloom,
A zephyr whispers, dismissing gloom.
In your eyes, a world I see,
Carried away by ecstasy.

Beneath the sky, devoid of sorrow,
We bask in dreams of sweet tomorrow.
Each gentle breeze, a lover's kiss,
In zephyr's flow, we find our bliss.

As twilight falls, unveiling night,
We dance in shadows, bathed in light.
Bound by whispers soft and true,
In ecstasy, I find you.

Firewater Embrace

Flickers ignite a hidden stream,
Melding in a fervent dream.
Heat and coolness intertwined,
Unity no one can unbind.

Rivers glow in fiery grace,
Flames reflect on water's face.
Whispers of the blaze and tide,
In this dance, worlds collide.

Liquid and flame in close array,
Turning night into day.
Passions merge, becoming whole,
Embers and waves console.

Sparkling Currents

Glittering flecks on restless flow,
In moonlight's silver glow.
Ripples shine in rhythmic beat,
A dazzling, moving sheet.

Each droplet holds a starry gleam,
Softly weaving through the stream.
Night's serenity embraced,
By current's radiant haste.

Flowing light in endless spree,
An evening symphony.
Harmony of waves and night,
Sparkling currents pure delight.

Dancing Waves

Graceful arcs in fluid motion,
An endless, rhythmic ocean.
Twisting, turning with finesse,
Nature's ballet in progress.

Waves caress the sandy shore,
Whispering of tales and lore.
Unseen fingers twirl and spin,
Where the dance does begin.

Underneath the sky so vast,
Effortless and unsurpassed.
Dancing waves in joyful spree,
Boundless in their symphony.

Fluid Enthusiasm

Rushing streams with fervent zest,
In their ceaseless quest.
Rolling, tumbling in delight,
Chasing day and kissing night.

Boundless in their liquid cheer,
Bubbling laughter we hold dear.
Eager currents race ahead,
In nature's path they're led.

Joy found in each fleeting drop,
Never pausing, never stop.
Fluid enthusiasm flows,
In rivers where the spirit grows.

Aqua Affection

In waves of blue, my heart does sway,
Underneath the moonlit bay.
Gentle tides, your touch entices,
In your depths, my love arises.

Silent whispers through the foam,
Guide my soul back to its home.
Every drop, a silver kiss,
In your arms, I find my bliss.

Crystal streams of pure affection,
Flow in perfect, clear connection.
In your currents, I confide,
Aqua love, forever tied.

Flood of Sentimentality

Memories surge like morning mist,
In pools of hope, I'm gently kissed.
Ebbing tides of time recall,
All the moments, big and small.

Overflows of cherished days,
In ocean's grasp, we're in a daze.
Waves of laughter, tears combined,
In this flood, our hearts entwined.

Eternal flow of past and present,
Drenched in love that's ever pleasant.
In the flood, we find our peace,
Sentimental tides, never cease.

Billows of Desire

Across the sea of midnight dreams,
Where passion flows in vivid streams.
Billows rise within our gaze,
Igniting love in fervent blaze.

The ocean's sighs, in rhythm joined,
Our longing hearts, they quite purloined.
In the dark, we burn as one,
Billows high till night is gone.

Desire's flame, a wild tide,
In your depths, I choose to bide.
Together in the storm we'll ride,
Billows strong with love inside.

Vortex of Emotion

In the whirl of tender feeling,
Caught within love's endless wheeling.
Spirals twist with no commotion,
In the vortex of emotion.

Through love's storm, I'm gently spun,
Underneath the burning sun.
Caught within your warm embrace,
In this spin, I find my place.

Hearts entwined in endless motion,
Lost within this deep devotion.
In the vortex, endlessly,
Our emotions set us free.

Rushing Love

In the quiet of midnight's call,
Hearts collide, barriers fall.
A pulse beneath the moonbeams,
Whispering shared dreams.

Eyes meet with an intense fire,
Burning with unspoken desire.
Time halts in love's embrace,
Rushing, soft and grace.

Hands entwined like ancient vines,
Tracing futures in invisible lines.
Silent vows in the cold air,
Swearing a fate to forever share.

Lover's bond, both bold and shy,
Stars reflected in their sigh.
Eternal promises softly spoken,
A love that will never be broken.

Deep Tide

Waves crashing on the distant shore,
Secrets lost, forevermore.
Moonlight's kiss on rippling seas,
A dance with a gentle breeze.

Depths unknown, a love so wide,
Carrying dreams on each tide.
Twilight hues blend and merge,
Two hearts bound in an ocean surge.

Currents strong, a force unseen,
Pulling together, serene.
In the heart of endless night,
Love's beacon, shining bright.

Ship set sail on destiny's course,
Guided by an unseen force.
In the vast, uncharted blue,
A love that's pure and true.

Brimming Passion

Flames that flicker in the dark,
Ignite the tender, hidden spark.
Beneath the stars, their spirits rise,
In the reflection of lover's eyes.

Trembling touch, electric feel,
Every caress, a love so real.
In the world, they find their place,
Two hearts in a passionate embrace.

Desire's whisper, a sweet herald,
In the core, a love unfurled.
Each heartbeat, a rhythmic beat,
In their love, they are complete.

Beyond the shadows, they reside,
In a sanctuary they confide.
Every moment, a boundless treasure,
In brimming passion, endless pleasure.

Effervescent Love

Bubbles rise in sparkling light,
Dancing in the velvet night.
Laughter rings, a cherished sound,
In effervescent joy, they are found.

Moments shared, like fleeting air,
In soft whispers, love's laid bare.
Eyes that glimmer, pure delight,
Hearts entwined, spirits bright.

Soft caresses, gentle and kind,
In their touch, a love defined.
With each breath, a promise anew,
In the glow, feelings true.

In every glance, they see the stars,
Tracing constellations in their scars.
Effervescent love soars high,
Boundless, reaching sky.

Waves of Sentiment

Upon the shores of memory bright,
The waves of sentiment take flight.
Whispers of old tales they carry,
In each moment, feelings tarry.

Echoes of a distant past,
In the waves, emotions cast.
Rolling over sands of time,
Rhythms of life in perfect rhyme.

Laughter mingles with the foam,
Sorrows find a fleeting home.
Every crest and every trough,
Gentle, tender, never rough.

In the vast expanse they play,
Through the night and through the day.
Caressing shores with soft embrace,
Waves of sentiment interlace.

For in their depths, stories blend,
And to the heart, solace send.
Ever moving, ever free,
In their dance, pure harmony.

A Stream of Delight

Glimmering beneath the moon's bright glow,
A stream of delight begins to flow.
Murmuring songs of purest grace,
It carves a path, a tender trace.

Through the meadows, past the trees,
It carries whispers on the breeze.
Crystals of joy within its gleam,
Reflecting dreams, a hopeful beam.

Flora drinks from this sweet course,
Nature's bounty, life's own source.
In its ripples, joy is found,
Harmonies of heart resound.

Dancing over stones so light,
Its rhythms bring the soul delight.
Ever onward, never still,
Flowing gently, pure goodwill.

For in its waters, life does spring,
A stream of delight, a gentle fling.
Endless journey, bright and clear,
Bringing happiness near, so near.

Surge of Tenderness

In the hush of twilight's fall,
A surge of tenderness does call.
With every heartbeat, whispers dear,
Caressing softly, drawing near.

Eyes that meet in silent gaze,
Filled with love, a warm embrace.
Moments stolen, moments shared,
In these seconds, hearts are bared.

The world falls away, so still,
In this space, the heart does fill.
With every touch, with every sigh,
Tenderness, a sweet reply.

Lips that speak in gentle tone,
Promises on which to hone.
Kindness wraps around the soul,
In this surge, we find our whole.

Bound by love, by softest care,
In this surge, all we dare.
To love, to hold, to never part,
In this tenderness, we start.

Rippled Hearts

Beneath the stars so high above,
Our rippled hearts in rhythm move.
Silent whispers, unspoken dreams,
In this moment, love redeems.

Like ripples on a tranquil lake,
Every beat, a soft quake.
Touching depths with gentle care,
We find each other everywhere.

In laughter's echo, joy is spun,
In tears, compassion, two as one.
Through the calm and through the storm,
Our rippled hearts, ever warm.

As moonlight dances on the wave,
In our love, we find the brave.
Journey through the night and day,
Together, come what may.

For in each ripple, trust is sown,
In every heartbeat, love is grown.
Rippled hearts that intertwine,
Bound forever, yours and mine.

Gush of Sentiment

Emotions ebb, flow with gentle might,
In twilight's soft, embracing light,
Sweet whispers carried on the breeze,
A heart's deep yearning, put at ease.

In tidal waves of joyous cries,
Where laughter breaks, where sorrow dies,
Each moment like a fleeting sigh,
Beneath the ever-changing sky.

We ride on currents swift and free,
Beneath the stars, just you and me,
Our transient sorrows washed away,
In dawn's first light, the break of day.

With passion's tide, we intertwine,
Two souls, one journey, so divine,
In love's vast ocean, wide and deep,
A promise in the waves we keep.

So let the river gently flow,
Through valleys high and fields below,
In every surge, a story told,
Of hearts entwined, forever bold.

Sweeping Romance

In gardens where the roses bloom,
Two hearts find shelter in the gloom,
With tender words and soft caress,
The world is painted with finesse.

A dance beneath the moonlit sky,
Whispers of love, the night's lullaby,
Through shadows cast by silver beams,
We chase the echoes of our dreams.

The gentle breeze that stirs the night,
Carries our love, pure and bright,
In every glance, a story told,
Of feelings fervent, fierce, and bold.

As stars align in cosmic grace,
We find our place in time and space,
With every kiss, a timeless pact,
A vow that binds, a love intact.

So let the night unveil its charm,
In each embrace, we find our calm,
With hearts that beat in perfect rhyme,
We'll conquer all, outlast the time.

Torrential Love

When stormy skies above us roar,
Our love remains, a beacon sure,
With every clash, our spirits rise,
Two hearts in tempest, bold and wise.

Through thunder's cry and lightning's flare,
We stand as one, beyond compare,
In torrents wild, our souls entwine,
A love unyielding, pure, divine.

No tempest fierce, no gale so strong,
Can mar the bond where we belong,
In rain's embrace, we find our truth,
An endless, vibrant, steadfast youth.

With every gust that shakes the night,
Our love grows stronger, burning bright,
In every storm, a pledge renewed,
A love that thrives in tempest's brood.

So let the heavens break and weep,
In love's embrace, our spirits keep,
Together through the storm we'll stand,
Our torrential love, forever grand.

A River's Yearning

In whispered dreams, the river flows,
Through valleys deep, where twilight glows,
It tells a tale of love divine,
Of hearts that seek, in shadows pine.

The waters murmur soft and sweet,
As lovers by the banks do meet,
With every tide, a longing heard,
In silent echoes, love is stirred.

By moonlit paths, the river winds,
Through tangled woods and ancient pines,
It carries wishes, dreams untold,
In every ripple, secrets hold.

The gentle stream, a wistful sigh,
Reflecting stars in midnight sky,
A mirror of the heart's desire,
To find its match, its endless fire.

So on it flows, through nights and days,
In search of love's eternal gaze,
A river's yearning, ever true,
A quest for hearts both old and new.

A Symphony of Love

In the silent night, hearts keep the beat,
Soft whispers of love, a melody sweet.
Stars dance above, in rhythmic delight,
Composing a symphony throughout the night.

Hands intertwine, a harmonious tune,
Beneath the graceful light of the moon.
Eyes speak volumes, words left unspoken,
A bond of two souls, beautifully woven.

Love's lullaby in every embrace,
Tender moments leave a gentle trace.
Together they stand, strong and free,
Their symphony of love, an endless sea.

Melodies linger in the morning dew,
Promises made for hearts to renew.
Each note of love pure, complete,
In this symphony, two hearts meet.

Surge of Emotions

A wave of joy sweeps through the heart,
Moments of bliss, a perfect start.
Deep in the core, emotions surge,
A canvas where colors gently merge.

Tides of laughter, ripples of grace,
The gentle touch of a loving face.
Boundless affection, endlessly deep,
Memories to cherish, moments to keep.

The heart beats strong, a pulse of fire,
A dance of passion, never to tire.
Dreams entwine, in the depths they swim,
In this surge of emotions, life begins.

Turbulent seas calm with a glance,
In love's tender embrace, a chance.
To ride the waves with steadfast devotion,
In this surge of powerful emotion.

Torrent of Affections

Rushing waters of passion and care,
A torrent of affections, beyond compare.
Every drop a kiss, every splash a touch,
In this flood of love, there's never too much.

Streams of kindness, rivers of grace,
Flowing freely, a warm embrace.
In the torrent's grasp, no fear, no pain,
Just the pure essence of love's reign.

Hearts overflow, like a broken dam,
In this torrent of affections, they slam.
Against the barriers of doubt and fear,
Love's powerful waters draw them near.

Beneath the surface, currents strong,
Drag them in a love where they belong.
In the torrent of affections, they find their place,
A love that's eternal, full of grace.

Currents of Longing

Winds whisper secrets through the trees,
Currents of longing, sail through the breeze.
Hearts yearning, searching wide,
In the flow of love, they confide.

Eyes meet across a crowded room,
In that moment, desires bloom.
Time stands still, just a fleeting glance,
In those currents, they take a chance.

The call of love, a distant shore,
Pulls them in, they want more.
In the depths, they dive so deep,
In the currents of longing, secrets keep.

Oceans apart, yet hearts entwined,
In every thought, the other they find.
Currents carry them, though miles away,
In longing's embrace, they forever stay.

Rivers of Desire

Through hills and dales, their course they steer,
In whispering currents, secrets near.
With longing rush, their waters flow,
To lands unknown, forgotten years.

A siren's call in moonlit nights,
They carve their path with gentle might.
Desires lost in shadows' dance,
Their song enchants, hearts ignite.

Frothing waves of passion's storm,
In restless sleep, they make their form.
On distant shores, their dreams alight,
In silhouettes of twilight's charm.

Over stones, through veils of mist,
In lovers' eyes, they softly twist.
Eternal streams from ancient springs,
Their touch, a tender, loving tryst.

Boundless journey, timeless flow,
In rivers' depths, our spirits grow.
Desire's course, a fate embraced,
In liquid veins, our love bestows.

Tides of Euphoria

With ebb and flow, a joyous swell,
In tidal waves, their stories tell.
A dance of light on waters wide,
The heart's embrace where hope can dwell.

In silver beams of moonlit glow,
Euphoria's tides begin to show.
They lift the soul to distant skies,
Where dreams in liquid stardust grow.

Crashing waves of laughter ring,
In ocean's song, our spirits sing.
Awash with joy, the world's renew,
With every tide, a blessing bring.

Upon the shores of morning's light,
They cast their spell, a pure delight.
A waltz of waves through endless time,
In every crest, our bliss ignite.

Whispers soft in ocean's breeze,
They carry dreams across the seas.
Tides of euphoria, ever near,
In their embrace, our sorrows cease.

A Stream of Yearning

Through forests deep, their whispers slide,
In gentle flow, where dreams reside.
A stream of yearning, soft and clear,
Where hearts converge, and worlds collide.

In dappled light of sunlit glades,
They trace a path in shadowed shades.
Their murmurings in silence weep,
Of love that's lost, yet never fades.

The ripples kiss the pebbled shore,
With sighs that ache forevermore.
A stream of wishes, boundless, true,
In every drop, a longing soar.

Through valleys green, their songs resound,
In every turn, desire is found.
A ceaseless quest for love's embrace,
Each bend a hope, in circles wound.

In twilight's veil, their murmurs blend,
Where yearning streams in rivers mend.
A tender plea, through time, it streams,
In waters' depths, our spirits send.

Ocean's Embrace

Beneath the stars, the waters span,
In ocean's arms, where dreams began.
With every wave, a whispered kiss,
A love so vast, no earthly plan.

The moonlit tides in secrets keep,
In depths profound, where shadows sleep.
Their tender pull, a siren's call,
To hearts adrift in longing sweep.

In ocean's depth, a world unknown,
Her touch, a solace, deep and lone.
A cradle of eternal night,
In waves' embrace, we find our home.

With gentle swells, they soothe the soul,
In rhythm's dance, a healing whole.
The ocean's song, a lullaby,
That mends the wounds and makes us whole.

Endless horizon, boundless grace,
In ocean's touch, our fears erase.
With every tide, a love's caress,
In ocean's arms, we find our place.

Misty Emotions

In the haze where feelings brew,
Gentle whispers softly coo.
Drops of rain on fragile hearts,
Life plays scenes in dusky parts.

Clouds conceal what words can't say,
Silent moments spliced with gray.
A tender touch, an unseen hand,
Guides us through a misty land.

Embers glow where shadows stray,
Hope emerges in the fray.
Balmy echoes soothe the night,
Misty dreams take silent flight.

Eyes reflect a soulful tide,
Hidden truths we can't abide.
In the mist, we find our way,
Through emotions, come what may.

Stars blink out, and dawn will rise,
Clearing up our clouded skies.
Through the mist, our hearts regain,
All the warmth dispelling pain.

Velvet Flood

Gentle tides of crimson flow,
Through the veins where passions go.
Under moonlight's tender grip,
Velvet rivers softly slip.

Waves caress the yearning shore,
Echoes whisper nevermore.
Sands dissolve in liquid grace,
Night's embrace, a soft embrace.

Carmine swirls in silent dance,
In the depths of sweet romance.
Ebb and flow of tender nights,
Fuels the dreams of our delights.

Rays of dawn break tender ties,
Velvet flood beneath the skies.
Colors bleed into the day,
Tracing paths where love will stay.

Hearts align within the stream,
Flowing gently like a dream.
Velvet flood, unending song,
Carries us where we belong.

Gush of Love

Pulses quicken, hearts ignite,
Love's cascade in endless flight.
Rivers of emotions blend,
In your eyes, I find my friend.

Torrent kisses, passion's bloom,
Filling every quiet room.
Every touch, a wave so strong,
Sweeping us where we belong.

Feelings rush in wild array,
Gush of love, come what may.
Winds of change can't quell the fire,
Burning bright with pure desire.

Mystic currents pull us near,
Swirling in a sea so clear.
Anchored by this fierce refrain,
Love's sweet rush we can't contain.

Endless depths in which we fall,
Gush of love envelops all.
Every beat, a testament,
To the love that's heaven-sent.

Roaring Affection

Thunderous hearts in synchrony,
Roaring love, fierce symphony.
Every beat a tidal wave,
Sweeping us, so strong, so brave.

Passions clash with fervent might,
Echoes roar into the night.
Every whisper, every sigh,
Roaring love just won't deny.

Fire dances in our gaze,
Roaring through the smoky haze.
Fury turned to gentle flame,
Roaring love in passion's name.

Storms that rattle can't abate,
Roaring love will not be sate.
Crescendos build in wild refrain,
Roaring love, where we remain.

Heartbeats drum a wild ride,
Roaring flow that won't subside.
In your eyes, I see the storm,
Roaring love, forever warm.

Blazing Cascade

Upon the mountains high and steep,
A fiery stream starts its leap.
Blazing trails in twilight's float,
A cascade burning, wild and remote.

Rocks whisper secrets to the flame,
In the night, they sing its name.
Through forest dark, its light extends,
A fevered dance that never bends.

Embers fly in glowing flight,
Stars reflect its blazing might.
Earth and fire in a fierce embrace,
Nature's spectacle, a surging grace.

Wind it meets with roaring sound,
Painting gold the forest ground.
In this dance of wild decree,
Nature's power, fierce and free.

At dawn it fades, and shadows play,
Whispers tell of night's display.
Blazing cascade now at rest,
In whispered tales, its fires invest.

Sweeping Hearts

Love's first glance, a gentle sweep,
In quiet corners, secrets keep.
Silent wishes take their flight,
Hearts are swept into the night.

Starlit paths and hidden ways,
Tender whispers softly graze.
In the hush of night's embrace,
Sweeping hearts in gentle chase.

Hands entwined, the tactful touch,
Moments linger, meaning much.
Eyes that speak in silent tone,
Lovers in a world unknown.

Winds of fate in twilight calm,
Carry dreams on tender palm.
Sweeping hearts through time and space,
Bound together in love's grace.

Endless skies and moonlit streams,
Love is born in whispered dreams.
Sweep of hearts in perfect tune,
Dancing 'neath the silver moon.

Ember Rapids

In the depth of forest dense,
Flows a river, swift and tense.
Ember rapids ebb and flow,
Streaks of fire, an urgent glow.

Rushing wild, it carves the ground,
Nature's pulse, a roaring sound.
Blazing paths through rock and stone,
Ancient secrets subtly sown.

Trees lean close, their branches bright,
Glimmering in the firelight.
In the river's fervent race,
Words of fire in loud embrace.

Currents strong, unyielding force,
Guiding nature on its course.
In the heart of twilight's glow,
Ember rapids fiercely flow.

As the night it softly ends,
Embers whisper to their friends.
Rapids calm under the sky,
Nature's lullaby and sigh.

Emotional Stream

In the quiet of the night,
Flows a stream of pure delight.
Emotions dance on waters clear,
Whispers close and always near.

Dreams converge on gentle waves,
Silent sorrows, joy that saves.
Through the stream, emotions blend,
Memories both foe and friend.

Tears that glisten, hearts that mend,
In this stream where love transcends.
Laughter's echo, sorrow's hue,
Feelings paint the water blue.

Every ripple tells a tale,
Love's endeavor, life's travail.
In the moonlight, shadows play,
Emotional stream guides the way.

Through the valleys deep and wide,
Where hearts and waters both collide.
In this stream of life's extremes,
Flowing free with endless dreams.

Energy Unleashed

In the heart of the storm, lightning roars,
Unleashing power, breaking doors,
Through shadow and light, it soars,
A force of nature, evermore.

Mountains bow, rivers plead,
To the boundless energy freed,
A symphony of strength indeed,
In every whisper, every reed.

Beyond horizons, it finds its path,
Unyielding in its feral wrath,
Yet gentle in its aftermath,
Etching stories on nature's graph.

With each gust and mighty quake,
The very earth begins to wake,
In its pulse, no calm to fake,
Only transformation, for heart's sake.

In every breath, a spark resides,
In every heart where courage hides,
From inner depths, this force abides,
Unleashing worlds in changing tides.

Pulse of Euphoria

A heartbeat in the silence pure,
A rhythm that none can ignore,
Echoes of joy, fresh and sure,
In every pulse, emotions pour.

Dancing lights in twilight's hold,
Stories in the stars retold,
Feelings cast in hues of gold,
Euphoria's grasp, gentle but bold.

In the whisper of the dawn,
Where dreams take flight, so well drawn,
A promise of a brighter morn,
In its pulse, pain is gone.

Through laughter that sweeps the night,
In eyes that shine with pure delight,
Euphoria dances in the light,
A symphony, perfect and bright.

Hold close the beat that never fades,
In every heart where hope cascades,
A pulse where memories are made,
In which all sorrows are unlaid.

Waves of Longing

In the quiet of twilight's bliss,
A feeling deep, a gentle kiss,
Memories surge, hard to dismiss,
In waves of longing, pure abyss.

Shadows stretch where sunlight fades,
In the heart where sorrow pervades,
Stories etched in time's cascades,
In longing's grip, all joy degrades.

Ocean's call, a whispered plea,
Across the waves, across the sea,
A yearning deep, wild and free,
For what was lost, what could be.

In the moon's reflective glow,
Silent tears in rivers flow,
Echoes of the past bestow,
A longing only few can know.

Between each breath, a sigh expressed,
In the heart where dreams confess,
A hope that time will ever bless,
Waves of longing, in tenderness.

Surge of Feelings

Beneath the stars, the night awakes,
A surge of feelings, the heart partakes,
In gentle whispers, silence breaks,
A melody of what it stakes.

Through veins of hope and fear it slides,
Across the tides of love it rides,
In shadows where the truth resides,
Feelings rise like unseen tides.

In every tear and every smile,
Moments linger for a while,
A surge of feelings to beguile,
Tracing hearts in timeless style.

The wind that carries secrets deep,
Feelings in its whispers keep,
Through dreams where lovers softly sleep,
A surge of feelings, vast and steep.

In every heartbeat, echoes play,
Words unspoken find their way,
Feelings rise as night meets day,
In endless surge, they softly sway.

Torrents of Desire

Beneath the silent, moonless night,
Where whispers merge with shadows' flight,
A tempest stirs, a longing fire,
In torrents deep, our hearts aspire.

The wind caresses tender skin,
Unveiling secrets held within,
Passion's wave, a boundless sea,
In fervent arms, we find we're free.

Stars above, their light embrace,
Illuminates our sacred space,
In this dance, pure hearts conspire,
To kindle flames, desire's choir.

The murmur of your gentle sighs,
Echoes in the night's reprise,
A symphony, each touch so dire,
Composed in torrents of desire.

Eyes that gleam with boundless hope,
In their depths, together cope,
Through storm and calm, we dare inquire,
Enveloped in these torrents of desire.

Rivers of Zeal

Across the plains where mountains tread,
Flows a river, life's thread,
In its course, bold dreams reveal,
The untamed surge of rivers of zeal.

Golden dawn breaks, skies ablaze,
Echoing our fervent gaze,
Each swift current, hand in hand,
We brave the wild, a boundless land.

With heartbeats loud as thunder's roar,
Together we, forevermore,
Chart our path, fierce and surreal,
Along the winding rivers of zeal.

In twilight's soft, impending glow,
Where distant dreams begin to show,
We venture forth with hearts so real,
Fueled by the endless rivers of zeal.

Through ebb and flow, we shall persist,
With every wave, each tender kiss,
Unyielding fire, our destiny we seal,
In the embrace of rivers of zeal.

Streams of Arousal

In twilight's whispered, fleeting grace,
Where shadows dance, our fingers trace,
Each secret touch, a stream so subtle,
Aroused by love's enchanting shuttle.

Soft murmur of a crescent moon,
Its glow reflects a tender tune,
Our hearts align, in synchrony,
In these streams of arousing harmony.

The night, a canvas, pure and dark,
We paint with sparks, igniting marks,
Sensations flow, relentless tide,
In streams of arousal, we reside.

Beneath the veil of starry skies,
A look, a touch, no sweet disguise,
Our souls entwine, pure thoughts unravel,
Within the streams of our arousal.

Each moment held in soft embrace,
Our love's caress, a sacred grace,
Together now, we deeply travel,
Along the streams of pure arousal.

Cascades of Ardor

In forests deep, where shadows lie,
Echoes of our hearts defy,
Each whispered word, our souls ignite,
In cascades of ardor, love takes flight.

Sunlight glints through canopy,
Glimmering our fantasy,
With every step, the passion soars,
In ardent cascades, evermore.

Through mossy trails and ancient stone,
Our spirits joined, we're never lone,
Raptured by this fervent stream,
Cascades of ardor, a shared dream.

The waterfall's embrace so wild,
A force untamed, yet soft and mild,
Our love pours forth, a sweet accord,
In these cascades, our hearts' reward.

With every breath, our fusion grows,
In every glance, affection shows,
Embracing now, with none ignored,
In cascades of ardor, deeply poured.

Unbridled Waters

Beneath the azure sky, they flow,
With secrets whispered, soft and low,
Rippling tales of places gone,
Their endless journey carrying on.

Mountains high and valleys deep,
Persistent waters, never sleep,
Carving paths through rock and stone,
In their wake, life's seeds are sown.

Moonlit nights and sunlit days,
In their dance, they weave and sway,
Waters rushing, wild and free,
To the depths of the boundless sea.

Voiceless echoes, hidden song,
In their course, they surge along,
Mystery in each wave and whirl,
Capturing dreams as they unfurl.

With power fed by rain and tear,
They flow through time, both far and near,
Unbridled waters, ageless might,
Their journey endless, out of sight.

Surging Essence

Life unearths its vibrant grace,
In the rhythm of a silent pace,
Essence drawn from earth's own heart,
Life in motion, from the start.

Unseen forces guide the way,
In the night and through the day,
Veins of nature, wild and grand,
Fingers tracing earth and sand.

Bound by naught but sky and stone,
Never captive, never alone,
Rushing forward, unrestrained,
Every drop a freedom gained.

Dancing shadows, morning light,
Essence surges, taking flight,
Cascading whispers, nature's song,
Joining forces, pure and strong.

Endless in its fervent quest,
Surging essence finds no rest,
Boundless spirit, fierce and free,
Marking time with wild decree.

Thrilling Stream

From the highlands, swift and clear,
Leaping forth without a fear,
Thrilling stream, so wild and bright,
Dances in the silver light.

Through the forest, past the glen,
Whispering secrets now and then,
Tumbling o'er the craggy rock,
Sparkling in its lively frock.

Voices join in harmony,
Stream and forest, wild and free,
Echoes rise in joyful chord,
Nature's symphony restored.

Leaves and petals ride the crest,
Where the water finds its rest,
Carried on with gentle grace,
In this untamed, joyous place.

Thrilling stream of constant cheer,
In your paths, our hearts revere,
Boundless beauty, swift and true,
Life's exhilaration, ever new.

Pulsating River

In the heart of the land it beats,
Throbbing rhythm, endless feats,
Pulsating river, full of life,
Carrying dreams and easing strife.

Flowing strong through night and day,
Guiding waters on their way,
Every turn a story told,
Mysteries in currents bold.

Beneath the stars, beneath the sun,
Rivers pulse, their spirits run,
Winding paths from source to sea,
Life's own rhythm, wild and free.

In its depths, life teems and thrives,
From its pulse, the world derives,
Nature's bloodline, moving fast,
Binding future, present, past.

Pulsating river, ceaseless flow,
In your paths, our stories grow,
Ever onward, ever strong,
In your journey, we belong.

Ebullient Waves

With light so bright, the morning sings,
As joy awakens, hearts take flight.
Ebullient waves bring joyous springs,
In rhythmic dance of pure delight.

The ocean's voice, a melody,
Where laughter blends with whispered breeze.
Each wave a note of harmony,
A symphony upon the seas.

Sunlight glitters on the crest,
Reflecting dreams that never fade.
In every surge, our hopes confessed,
As stars align, and futures made.

Ebullient waves, with endless cheer,
Transform the shore to realms of gold.
Where every heart can persevere,
And tales of wonder thus unfold.

So let us ride the waves of glee,
Embracing life with passion's spark.
For in the ebullient, we see,
A world ignites through light and dark.

Cascade of Tenderness

A cascade flows from heart to heart,
In whispers soft, our tales conveyed.
Where tenderness in artful part,
In gentle ripples, dreams are laid.

Each droplet speaks of love's embrace,
A language pure in liquid form.
And in this stream, we find our place,
A refuge safe, a haven warm.

With every flow, a thousand hues,
Reflecting all that we hold dear.
A tender touch beneath the blues,
In waters bright, the skies so clear.

The cascade's song, a soothing balm,
That mends the wounds of yesteryears.
It cradles time in peaceful calm,
Dissolving all our deepest fears.

Oh, let us drift on tender streams,
Where hearts can heal and souls unite.
In cascades rich with gentle dreams,
We'll weave our love in endless light.

Waters of Affection

In waters deep, affection blooms,
A garden found beneath the wave.
Where every current softly looms,
And every whisper finds its grave.

So tender, soft, the stream unfurls,
A tapestry of silken threads.
It carries love in hidden swirls,
In paths where every heart is led.

Through eddies fine, our spirits meld,
In quiet dance beneath the sun.
With every flow, a tale is held,
Of love's sweet course that's just begun.

The waters speak in gentle tones,
Of memories etched in liquid gold.
In every drop, our journey hones,
A story waiting to be told.

Let's sail upon these waves of grace,
Where love's affection knows no end.
In waters pure, our hearts embrace,
As boundless streams of love transcend.

Swells of the Soul

In swells of soul, our spirits rise,
On waves that touch the boundless sky.
Where dreams take flight and seldom die,
In endless azure, hopes belie.

Within the heart, a storm will brew,
With passions wild, and courage strong.
Each swell of soul brings forth the new,
In currents deep, where we belong.

The ocean's vast, a mirror bright,
Reflecting all our inner tides.
In every crest, we seek the light,
That through the tempest, safely guides.

Our souls do dance in ocean's sway,
Embracing all that life bestows.
In ev'ry wave, the heart will play,
A symphony that ever grows.

So let us sail on swells of soul,
With faith and love as our decree.
In boundless seas, we'll find our role,
And ride the waves eternally.

Swells of Emotion

In twilight's gentle, somber glow,
Memories like rivers flow,
Heartbeats whisper soft and low,
In swells of emotion, feelings grow.

A dance of shadows, life's ballet,
Waltzing through both night and day,
With every pulse and every sway,
Emotions rise, then drift away.

Like tides that ebb and pulses roar,
A symphony on time's grand shore,
Echoes of what came before,
In whispered swells, we feel it more.

Beneath the stars' demure embrace,
Dreams awaken, find their place,
In swells of tender, endless grace,
Emotion's tide, we all must face.

So let the heart its cadence find,
In swells of thought and dreams entwined,
For in these waves, our souls aligned,
Eternal in this dance, defined.

Gushing Devotion

In depths of heart, where secrets lie,
Love's fierce torrent rushes by,
A flood of stars in night's dark sky,
A gush of devotion, spirits sigh.

Rivers of passion, wild and free,
Flow between both you and me,
In every glance, in every plea,
Gushing love for eternity.

Boundless waves, so strong and pure,
In devotion, hearts secure,
A steadfast love, we can endure,
In gushing streams, forever sure.

Embrace the flood of heartfelt dreams,
In moonlit nights where everything gleams,
Together in these endless streams,
Gushing devotion, so it seems.

Our hearts, a sea of endless grace,
In gushing love, we find our place,
Hand in hand, a tender embrace,
Devotion's flow, our souls enlace.

Quiet Streams

In fields where morning shadows play,
Quiet streams meander, sway,
With whispers of the dawn's new day,
In nature's song, they softly stay.

Gentle waters, clear and bright,
Reflect the early morning light,
A tranquil scene, a peaceful sight,
In quiet streams, our hearts delight.

Wandering through the forest green,
With thoughts as calm as they have been,
In tranquil moments, life is seen,
Through quiet streams, serene and keen.

In silence deep, we come to find,
A solace pure within the mind,
A gentle flow, our souls unwind,
In quiet streams, peace intertwined.

So let us wander, side by side,
Where quiet streams in stillness bide,
In nature's arms, we shall abide,
In gentle flow, our hearts confide.

Sentient Flow

In currents strong, the spirits weave,
A sentient flow, where dreams conceive,
Whispers in the night's reprieve,
In quiet thoughts, we all believe.

Through rivers deep and oceans wide,
In sentient flow, we often glide,
With every turn, and every stride,
The heart's own path, it does confide.

A dance of words, in thoughts that stream,
Through sentient flow, a living dream,
In every sigh, and silent theme,
The essence of life's gentle beam.

In twilight's frame, the story grows,
Through sentient flow, the truth bestows,
A journey where the spirit knows,
In endless rhythm, life's echoes.

So let us drift, in thought's embrace,
The sentient flow, a timeless space,
With every turn, we find our place,
In flowing dreams, a soft grace.

Uncontainable Whirl

Within the boundless dance, untamed and free,
Spirits ascend where the wind meets sea.
Colors swirl in a chaotically sweet trance,
Echoes of laughter in the cosmic expanse.

Stars ignite as dreams unfurl,
Moments cascade in a majestic whirl.
Time loops back in an endless twirl,
Uncontainable, a dancer in pearl.

Infinite turns where limits cease,
A crescendo built on timeless peace.
Breath suspended in sheer release,
Harmony finds its blessed lease.

Chasing shadows of the daylight's gleam,
The heart awakens from a fragile dream.
Life's essence flows in a radiant stream,
Uncontainable whirl, sweet and supreme.

Veins of Love

Through the veins of love, rivers flow,
A symphony of whispers, soft and low.
Hearts interlace where wildflowers grow,
In fields where tender feelings show.

Beneath the canopy, stars align,
Celestial sparks in a design.
Each heartbeat echoes, yours and mine,
Threads entwined in love's divine.

Roots dig deep in fertile ground,
A steadfast passion, ever found.
In every pulse, a love profound,
Eternal vows in silence crowned.

Winds may shift and seasons change,
Yet our bond no force can estrange.
Through life's open, boundless range,
Veins of love, forever arranged.

Sparkling Rush

Morning breaks with a glittering rush,
Awakening dreams in a singular hush.
Fresh drops of dew on petals blush,
A world's rebirth, no longer crushed.

Sunlit trails carve paths anew,
Golden beams in a sky so blue.
Whispers of dawn in the gentle dew,
Hope, an ember in a sparkling view.

The river sings in joyful pace,
Water's dance, a hurried grace.
Reflections burst in a mirrored space,
Light cascades, a nature's embrace.

Glorious rays in a radiant streak,
Each moment peaks with voices sleek.
Life's cadence in a sparkling tweak,
Euphoria in the rush we seek.

Vibrant Flood

In the vibrant flood of colors bright,
Radiance pierces through the night.
Waves of wonder in sheer delight,
Emerging hues in boundless flight.

Crimson, amber, shades of gold,
Stories of splendor, yet untold.
Brushstrokes fierce, yet uncontrolled,
A canvas of marvels to behold.

Blossoms bloom in fervent spree,
Nature's palette, wild and free.
Spectrum wide as the endless sea,
Drenched in vivid, luminous glee.

As the vibrant flood cascades in grace,
Time dissolves in its fervent pace.
Every shade holds a sacred space,
Life's art in an endless embrace.

Crashing Waves

In the realm of churning seas,
Rising tides with fervent plea,
Echo whispers of the breeze,
Nature's hymn, wild and free.

Crests that curl and fiercely pound,
Sending roars and thunderous sound,
Nature's temper, unbound,
With each clash, new paths are found.

Sunlight glints on watery peaks,
Tells of mysteries that they keep,
Where the deep unto us speaks,
In the heart of stormy sweep.

Shorelines kissed by salty breath,
Where relentless waves bequeath,
Stories spun in liquid depth,
Of life's dance, beyond belief.

In the dance of sea and sky,
Where they meet and say goodbye,
Crashing waves in rhythmic sigh,
Whisper secrets none deny.

Boundless Brook

Through the glen, a brook does wind,
Clear and cool in sun's warm shine,
Whispers tales, both old and kind,
Nature's wisdom intertwined.

Pebbles smooth beneath its flow,
Humming tunes that few may know,
Songs of times long ago,
In its endless, gentle go.

Mossy banks and shaded nooks,
Offer rest to those who look,
Into depths of boundless brooks,
Where life's tranquil paths are took.

Sunbeams dance on glistening waves,
Lighting paths which nature paves,
Timeless echoes from the cave,
Where the brook its solace craves.

Sorrows fall and joys arise,
In the brook's reflective eyes,
Boundless dreams beneath the skies,
Wrapped in waters' soft disguise.

Yearnful Tides

When the moon sings to the sea,
Tides arise in yearnful plea,
Carrying whispers meant to be,
Echoes of a wild decree.

Undulating dreams ascend,
From the ocean's timeless bend,
Yearnful tides on journeys send,
Messages to comprehend.

Silver beams on water's crest,
Guide the heart to seek its quest,
Yearning rhythms, never rest,
In the waves, forever blessed.

Love and loss etched in the foam,
Each returning tide finds home,
Yearnful hearts no more to roam,
Where the sea, as sky, is known.

Endless dance of ebb and flow,
Tales of ancient winds, they show,
In the tide's yearnful glow,
Life's eternal, gentle woe.

Heart Surge

In the quiet depth of night,
Where the stars emit soft light,
Surges hearts with keen delight,
Feelings bold, pure and bright.

Passion's waves break on the shore,
Echoes heard forevermore,
In the throb of love's rapport,
Mysteries of hearts explore.

Through the silence, whispers dart,
From the depths of longing heart,
In the surge, they find their part,
Soul and passion never part.

Rivers run with fervent pace,
In the heat of love's embrace,
ஞs of timeless, boundless grace,
ɜach heartbeat's lively race.

ℷ dawn begins to rise,
ᶠt glow, it magnifies,
ⁱns the morning skies,
ᵛf love's sunrise.

Roiling Enthusiasm

Beneath a sky of restless dreams,
A fervent pulse ignites the night.
The world awakes in vibrant gleams,
With every star, a flicker of delight.

The wind it roars with untamed song,
Its symphony in swirling flight.
Each leaf and branch it dances long,
Embracing dawn with purest might.

Passion stirs in hearts anew,
A fire that burns without respite.
In shades of gold and cobalt blue,
We chase our dreams, take fearless flight.

Through valleys deep and peaks so high,
This roiling force it leads the way.
With eager steps we touch the sky,
On paths where wild hopes brightly play.

As morning breaks with hues so wide,
We dive into the day's grand scheme.
With roiling enthusiasm as our guide,
We live within our truest dream.

Vivid Swirls

In the quiet of the morn,
Colors burst with sudden grace.
Vivid swirls of light reborn,
Paint the dawn with their embrace.

Crimson, violet, softest blue,
Glimmering in the early glow.
Each hue tells a tale anew,
Of whispered secrets we may know.

Brush of sunlight, tender touch,
Turns the world to living art.
In these swirls, there's magic such,
That binds the soul to nature's heart.

A dance of shadows, light entwined,
Creating realms of pure delight.
In every stroke, a design,
That fills our minds with endless sight.

As the day begins its flight,
Carrying dreams on painted streams.
We are caught in swirling light,
Carving paths of vivid dreams.

Ecstatic Flow

The river hums a vibrant tune,
Its waters gleam in sunlight's glow.
A dance beneath the silver moon,
In currents wild, an ecstatic flow.

Each wave a whisper, soft yet bold,
Carving tales in ancient stone.
Through fields of green and sands of gold,
It journeys free, forever flown.

Boundless, ceaseless in its quest,
It finds the path where none can see.
In every twist, in every crest,
A testament to being free.

Life itself in waters bright,
Chasing dreams in liquid flight.
With every bend, it finds new light,
In the flow, eternal right.

Nature's song in endless stream,
Echoing through time and space.
In ecstatic flow, we find the theme,
Of life's unconquerable grace.

Rushing Adoration

In the caress of morning breeze,
Whispers rush through fields of green.
Adoration flows with ease,
In nature's symphony serene.

The sun bestows its golden kiss,
On petals soft, on rivers wide.
In every ray, we find pure bliss,
Rushing through the changing tides.

Birds in flight sing joyous tune,
Their hearts alight with boundless love.
In every note, a sweet commune,
A rushing adoration from above.

Mountain peaks and valleys low,
Speak in silence of their grace.
Through their whispers, rivers flow,
In adoration's warm embrace.

As twilight falls and stars ignite,
Heaven's canvas, vast and free.
In rushing adoration's light,
We find the love that sets us free.

Twisting Emotions

Beneath the sky of changing hues,
Our hearts dance in a tangled muse.
Whispers of the night entwine,
In shadows deep, our fates align.

Torrent tears in moonlit showers,
Moments stretched like endless hours.
Fading light in morning's call,
Feelings twist, rise, then fall.

Paths unknown and steps so wary,
Voices soft, yet dreams so scary.
Twisting echoes in the breeze,
Longing hearts on bended knees.

Passions flaring with each turn,
In love's fire, we both burn.
Silent screams and hushed desires,
Twisting flames, heart aspires.

Through this maze, with hope we steer,
Twisting emotions, crystal clear.
In each other's eyes, we find,
The love that binds, the ties that bind.

Dashing Essence

In the mornings soft embrace,
Dashing essence sets the pace.
Whispers of a day unknown,
In sunlight's warmth, seeds are sown.

Fleeting moments in a rush,
Nature's paintbrush, sunrise blush.
Essence of a life so grand,
With every heartbeat, take a stand.

Quickly moving, time's decree,
Life's short dance, wild and free.
Dashing through the dreams we crave,
On the brink, but standing brave.

Shadows lengthen, die and fade,
Essence gleams where paths were laid.
Dashing soul in twilight's gleam,
Follow through the brightest dream.

Oceans whisper, mountains call,
Dashing essence, feel it all.
In the end, with stars we blend,
Essence dashing, never bend.

Loving Tide

Near the shore, where whispers play,
Loving tide comes, then drifts away.
In its pull, the heart does glide,
To realms where dreams and hopes reside.

Soft caress of love's embrace,
Tides of passion, full of grace.
As the moonlight guides the sea,
Loving tide, you carry me.

Ebb and flow, the gentle swing,
Of a love that's blossoming.
In each wave, a story told,
Loving tide, so warm and bold.

In the dusk or morning light,
We follow where the tide is right.
Hand in hand, through highs and lows,
Loving tide, where true love flows.

When the storm clouds fill the sky,
Loving tide will lift us high.
Through the waves, so strong and wide,
We journey on with loving tide.

Rhythmic Undercurrents

Beneath the surface, calm and still,
Rhythmic undercurrents thrill.
In the flow and gentle sway,
Secrets of the deep display.

Life's concerto in disguise,
Undercurrents harmonize.
In the depths of ocean's dance,
Every wave a second chance.

Feel the pulse within the deep,
Ancient rhythms softly weep.
Patterns etched in liquid stone,
Undercurrents, overtone.

Silent echoes, heartbeats blend,
Where sky and sea seem to mend.
Rhythmic whispers, shadows send,
A dance that time can't comprehend.

Journey through this liquid trance,
In the rhythm, hearts advance.
Undercurrents draw us in,
To where the soul and sea begin.

Luminous Waves

Beneath the silver moonlit glaze,
The ocean sighs in soft embrace.
Stars dance upon the gentle crest,
In night's serene and quiet grace.

Whispers of aquatic dreams,
Echo through the tidal streams.
Each ripple paints a fleeting tale,
On the canvas of moonbeams.

The depths reveal their hidden lore,
Where mysteries and myths explore.
Darkened abysses hold their sway,
Beneath the surface evermore.

A symphony of light and flow,
Where waves and moonlight gently glow.
The sea hums ancient lullabies,
From eons gone, yet still they grow.

In the cradle of the night,
The ocean mirrors stars so bright.
A harmony of glistening waves,
In nature's pure, exquisite rite.

Bursting Love

In every glance, a spark ignites,
A fire that warms the coldest nights.
Silent talks and knowing ways,
Unite two hearts in endless lights.

Emotions burst in vibrant hues,
Painting skies in lover's views.
Every touch, a whispered song,
A tender breath, a love that's true.

Hand in hand, they face the streams,
Of life's unpredictable schemes.
Together, strong through every storm,
In unison, they chase their dreams.

Each moment shared, a treasure rare,
In love's embrace, they find their air.
Through highs and lows, they stand as one,
A force that nothing can impair.

Their hearts beat in a rhythmic line,
An endless dance, a love divine.
Bursting forth with every day,
In perpetual, sweet entwine.

Swirling Zeal

Whirling, twirling, zestful flight,
Hearts ablaze with sheer delight.
Passion roars in stormy skies,
In fevered dance, they chase the light.

Enthusiasm guides their way,
Through every dark and dawn's bright ray.
With fervent hearts, they forge ahead,
In ardor's wild and fierce array.

Zealous winds propel their course,
Their spirits fueled by unseen force.
United in a single aim,
In life's grand tempest, they endorse.

Through trials and across vast fields,
Their zeal the strongest armor wields.
With burning eyes and open hearts,
They chase the dreams ambition yields.

In swirling zeal, they're ever driven,
By passion's call, their purpose given.
An endless surge of potent fire,
To live, to love, to thrive, and aspire.

Radiant Waters

Crystal clear, the waters gleam,
Reflecting sun's resplendent beam.
They dance in light, a vivid scene,
A daydream woven in a stream.

In radiance, the rivers flow,
Through valleys lush and meadows low.
The sunbeams kiss their surface bright,
In nature's gentle ebb and flow.

Beneath the shining, shimmering face,
Lie depths undisturbed and full of grace.
A world unseen, yet sparkling pure,
An endless, tranquil, flowing space.

The waters speak in silent verse,
In languages both grand and terse.
Their radiance a timeless tale,
Of life's unending, mystic course.

With every gleaming, glistening wave,
The radiant waters softly save,
A memory of light's embrace,
An ever-flowing, natural rave.

Current of Yearning

In yearning's stream, I cast my heart,
Emotions flow, cannot depart,
The current pulls, can't break apart,
Desires surge, a boundless chart.

Whispers ride the water's crest,
Memories nudge, granting no rest,
In longing's deep, I am a guest,
To fate's embrace, my soul addressed.

Dreams like waves, relentless sweep,
Passion's tide, both cold and deep,
In tender thoughts, my secrets keep,
Yearning's river, where spirits leap.

Among the reeds, where silence hums,
Echoes of love, my mind succumbs,
Hope's gentle breath, forever drums,
In currents wild, my heart benumbs.

Embrace the flow, with no return,
In love's embrace, forever yearn,
For in these depths, we live and learn,
In soulful tides, we passion churn.

Lustrous Rapids

Through the rapids, gleam and shine,
A love so fierce, it's near divine,
In every turn, we intertwine,
Lustrous rapids, bold design.

In cascades of a passion pure,
Flowing fast, yet ever sure,
In hearts like these, we find a cure,
Lustrous rapids, our love's allure.

Down the rocks, our spirits sweep,
In lustrous waves, our secrets keep,
Through luminous nights, we lose no sleep,
For love's bright rush, runs ever deep.

With every force, our hearts connect,
In rapids wild, no love neglect,
A gleaming path, our fates direct,
In lustrous flow, our joys reflect.

Let the river of love unfurl,
In rapids bright, our spirits swirl,
For in this rush, we find a pearl,
Lustrous rapids, love's true whirl.

Rushing Espirit

Rushing spirits, wild and free,
We dance upon a love's decree,
In every rush, a spark to see,
Espirit rules, our destiny.

By wind and wave, our hearts advance,
In the rush of a fervent trance,
To love's pure song, we both entrance,
In spirited flow, we take the chance.

Through torrents bold, we carve our path,
In rushing streams, we find our laugh,
With every surge, we face the wrath,
Yet love endures, in aftermath.

Espirit runs through veins of gold,
A tale of love that's finely told,
In rushing breaths, we feel the fold,
Of time's embrace, both young and old.

Let spirits rush, let hearts entwine,
In every pulse, a love divine,
For in this rush, true souls align,
Rushing espirit, ever shine.

Tempestuous Love

In the heart's stormy seas, we dwell,
Waves crash where secrets often tell,
Beneath lightning's fervent, sacred spell,
Passions rise where shadows fell.

With fervor's force, our spirits bind,
In tempests churn, no fears confined,
Amid the chaos, love we find,
A whirlwind dance, our souls entwined.

Through torrid gales, our laughter breaks,
Two hearts that beat, the storm awakes,
For in the fury, love remakes,
A fire that no deluge stakes.

Thunder roars through night's abyss,
A fleeting glance, a stolen kiss,
In storm's embrace, we find our bliss,
Tempestuous love, sweet as this.

Each tempest dawn, we're born anew,
With eyes like stars, and skies of blue,
In wild embrace, our hearts pursue,
A love untamed, forever true.

Rushing Hearts

In the rivers of time, our hearts collide,
Flowing swiftly where dreams reside,
Touch by touch, with nothing to hide,
In love's embrace, our spirits glide.

Beneath the moon, our whispers fly,
Carried on winds that kiss the sky,
With every breath, a gentle sigh,
As rushing hearts together lie.

In the torrent of passion's fate,
Two souls entwine, recalibrate,
Bound by love, we celebrate,
The pulse of life, accelerate.

Through valleys deep and mountains high,
Our hearts like eagles, ever nigh,
In storm and calm, 'neath clear blue sky,
Rushing hearts, to never die.

Forevermore, in currents' sweep,
Our love a river, wide and deep,
In dreams we wade, where secrets keep,
Rushing hearts, eternal leap.

Sweeping Affection

Through fields of gold, we roam so free,
Where love's sweet whisper, beckons me,
In every breeze, a melody,
A tune that sings of you and me.

With every step, our hearts align,
In tender grace, your hand in mine,
Affection's sweep, a sign divine,
Two souls as one, our spirits shine.

In twilight's glow, when day does end,
Our shadows merge, as if they blend,
In love's vast sweep, we comprehend,
The boundless joy, that hearts extend.

Under stars, in night's embrace,
Our love, a constant, gentle grace,
With sweeping affection, we find our place,
In each other's eyes, a treasured space.

Forever, let this love be pure,
A bond so strong, steadfast and sure,
In sweeping affection, we secure,
A love that's boundless, will endure.

Gushing Zeal

In every touch, our passion springs,
A fervent fire, that brightly clings,
To every word, our zeal it brings,
A love that soars, on ardent wings.

With fervor's rush, our spirits light,
In day and dark, through every night,
This gushing zeal, a pure delight,
Our hearts ablaze, with wondrous sight.

In whispering winds, our vows resound,
With fervid grace, our souls are bound,
In every heartbeat, love is found,
Gushing zeal, with no confound.

Through every storm, and calm serene,
A promise held, in eyes so keen,
With gushing zeal, our love's machine,
Together strong, a radiant sheen.

Forevermore, our hearts will blaze,
In tireless zeal, through all our days,
With gushing fervor, endless praise,
Our love in bright, eternal rays.

Milton Keynes UK
Ingram Content Group UK Ltd.
UKHW022248030824
446595UK00003B/73